THE
STENOGRAPHER'S
BREAKFAST

BARNARD NEW WOMEN POETS SERIES
Edited by Christopher Baswell and Celeste Schenck

THE
STENOGRAPHER'S
BREAKFAST

FRANCES McCUE

With an Introduction by
Colleen J. McElroy

BEACON PRESS   BOSTON

Beacon Press
25 Beacon Street
Boston, Massachusetts 02108-2892
www.beacon.org

Beacon Press books
are published under the auspices of
the Unitarian Universalist Association of Congregations.

First digital edition 2001

Library of Congress Cataloging-in-Publication Data
McCue, Frances.
The stenographer's breakfast / Frances McCue with an introduction by Colleen J. McElroy.
p.   cm. — (Barnard new women poets series)
ISBN 0-8070-6816-0 (cloth).
ISBN 0-8070-6817-9 (pbk.)
I. Title. II. Series
PS3563.C35275S74   1992
811'.54—dc20   91-41839

*For two friends who lead me
everywhere.*

Frances Blasdel Reardon
(1904–1981)

and

Mark Andrew Webster
(1960–1990)

CONTENTS

III. TRANSLATION

ACKNOWLEDGMENTS

Grateful acknowledgment is made to the editors of the journals in which these poems first appeared:

"In Single Moments," "Soundmaker," "Doctor Doctor," "Doubling Up on Privacy at the Canterbury Juvenile Facility," "Etiquette," "Barn Raising," and "Dead Reckoning" appeared in *Poetry Northwest.*

"What's Dangerous about Plumbing" and "According to Neophysics" appeared in *River City.*

One section of "In a Town Not Far from Here: Speeches from the Mayor's Office" appeared in *Onionhead.*

"Aunt Lillian, the Chemist and the Magician" is forthcoming in *Poetry Ireland Review.*

"The Princess and the Highwire" appeared in *Ergo! The Bumbershoot Literary Magazine.*

My thanks also to Colleen J. McElroy, Gary Greaves, Rob Roy Anderson, Jan Wallace, Paulann Petersen, Wendy Feuer, my parents, Peter and Mary-Gaines Standish, and to the stenographers who helped transcribe and inform.

INTRODUCTION

Colleen J. McElroy

One of my most memorable and least appealing jobs during my early graduate student years was as an assistant to the Government Documents librarian. There I learned the mysteries of classifications and designations assigned to the quagmire of government offices, divisions, departments, and committees. The Documents room was a small space clotted ceiling to floor with pale brown stacks of cardboard boxes, ragged piles of pamphlets, reports, and booklets, hundreds of boxes of file cards, and bins of letter shelves—all of it coated with an almost imperceptible layer of dust which gathered on a document the moment it entered the air of that room. But under that layer were records of governmental structures, national triumphs, political disasters, attempts to keep the nation solvent, and efforts to keep it democratic. My job was to file the mess before it all turned to mulch. Each day, I faced the unglamorous task of opening yet another box of paperwork spewed off the presses of the Government Printing Office and sent out for public dissemination. Each day, I coded parcels according to origin, class, subclass, docket, and year, all under an alphabetic cross-hatch of decimals, dashes, and numbers that forced me to think in a language that was completely nonfunctional outside of the confines of the Documents room. And all of this while regular library traffic swirled past the door and onto brighter subjects in the seemingly legible languages of law, literature, biology, and social subjects.

If I complained, the Documents librarian would say, "Don't worry. They have to come this way soon. We hold the key to all in this room." And she would gesture to the hodge-podge of pamphlets and treatises, the cartons of material waiting to be cataloged in the nearly indecipherable codes of class, caste, and purpose, some of it representing sections of government which would vanish more quickly than the ink on each card. Presented with the right request form, I translated those coded patterns and led readers to actual documents. I was, I suppose, a kind of stenographer of bureaucracy, coding the chaos of government affairs in what, at first glance, seemed to be no more than a collection of squiggly lines leading to the smoke and alchemy of business detailed in documents that held their own chaotic and arbitrary images.

Frances McCue pulls us into a similar world in *The Stenographer's Breakfast*. It is a world where chaos is created in a language that struggles with imagination bound by emotions, and with obedience to accuracy uncorrupted by emotions.

> *Shorthand:* a lack, understaffed, decoding and
> recoding, carrying language to its core.
>
> And more—the world of facts brought to
>   bear . . .
> Such faith I have in sounds not yet
> formed as words, shy riddles and intrusions . . .

Despite its *shy riddles,* McCue takes a hard look at the mechanized system of a society bent on literal interpretation, where emotions are cloaked and imagination is political.

> . . . This is the walk from the office
> when the keypunch and earphones
> shinny down my bones, and patter skin.
> Not long, and I can't distinguish between my
>   own

footfall and the street, my eye from market
or kiosk—I can't help transcribing

everything. . . .

With this sometimes caustic, sometimes sardonic eye, McCue
examines acculturation and survival. Her heroine is a sensible
Cinderella. No glass slipper or fancy ball, the stenographer
takes up the machines of modern efficiency, complete with the
problems of transcribing the literal dictates of society.

> Aside: *To take dictation* means I watch each
>   speak,
> turn my face, read lips and leap—*space*— . . .

It is those leaps that blur the neat parameters prescribed as
an antidote for chaos. Images seemingly are scattered through
the poems with the same abandonment as the symbols on a
stenographer's tape appear to an untrained eye. But through the
stenographer's eyes, we see the danger of sacrificing freedom for
order, and of disallowing language left emotionally loose. "How
can I help / loving the chronological / seductions of file and
box?" she asks. "Imagine the alternative chaos." But indeed, the
chaos exists, and it is the storm and dross of that chaos which
feeds this collection.

In Part I, Dictation, we see a glimpse of that chaos, a world
where imagination struts in and overturns all the furniture,
where flies disguise themselves as bees, and the princess is for-
ever bound to a highwire act of love and rejection—everything
here is in motion. That motion defies linearity and is in con-
flict with the parsimonious language of dictation. But transcrib-
ing the real world means first determining what is real, and
what is real is not always literal.

The stenographer's world is coded in a poetic reality that
sometimes distances, sometimes pulls the reader in for a close-
up shot. The princess ("The cast calls, longs for a princess.

Without her, the show / cannot go on."), scampering across the landscape of the highwire, is as much of the real and the imaginative world as the hangman ("To execute with the cool hand / of a programmer, I aim, then feel / the world as a series of knobs / or switches waiting for the flip by one / who knows no in-between, doesn't believe), or Aunt Lillian ("Upstairs, resourceful Aunt Lil / found the magician in the yellow pages/ when she looked under *maids*, / How tidy a magician would be—"). They are all trapped in designated roles in which they are expected to remain unemotional. For all of their proclamations and rationales, they are bound to the same landscape, a landscape that somehow does not match the expected even when the event is a common one.

> . . . One Easter, three of us
> had to bury
> a cat. In the city,
> we had only concrete, construction yards, or the
> park.
> We had children to think of, or the rain
> lifting the cat back
> to us, half-decayed.
> This death was a pun or wry little joke: we had
> particulars
> to consider . . .

In a literal world, one must be practical. In the Government Documents room, the head librarian wore no-nonsense shoes, English walking styles that matched her accent, and hair that never budged, no matter how often we frantically rushed to steady cardboard cartons that threatened to topple over and crush us both. She taught me codes that would hold up to anyone's scrutiny. And she brought me dishes of spicy curry, the most delicious I've tasted then or since, an art learned, she said, during her years with the "Home Office." Then she would promptly duplicate the rigors of that office in the Documents

Room. At the time, I marveled at how succulent dishes of curry could coexist in a woman whose mind seemed fixated on classification systems. But just as *"Time releases / the tower's clock from its confines,"* I have learned to imagine the librarian outside of her codes and decimal ratings. Her work required loyalty, the ability to produce steadfastly a system of uniform symbols that lead to clear, simple, and rational language. (All of this from government documents!) The art, her method of self-expression, came later and was more intuitive, more emotional. It was saved for that time between cataloging chores, a time when she reminisced. For small moments, she separated emotion from the "flip of the light switch / . . . some calculated truth." I only saw her once after I had fled that job—the top of her head bearly visible above the rows of unopened cardboard boxes. Not an unkind woman, but selfless and accurate to a fault, she might have been McCue's dictator's dream, her behavior as defined by the *dictator.*

> The day they carried her out, I was bending
> over her garden. Released, the winded flowers
> marched to their borders: little heads of steer,
> stubborn and slow. Wrapped in her dinner linens,
> she was still angled, seated as she was
> by the phone, borne across the lawn. How happy
> I was seeing her twirled up in her own
> etiquette, in *those cloths we save for company.*

What happens when the stenographer turns human and looks back, when she is "whisked into life behind / the retina, several times removed"? "My job is to look after things," she opines. *To look* implies not only tending to but looking *after* once the event is over, to see what is left, to wait until it has ended. In Part II, Transcription, we look after events, see their legacies and how they are tended to. "Doctor Doctor" urges "Wake wake wake-up / This is a house call." and obediently, we trek through the houses of memory, ill-fitting and familiar though they may be. "Going Back to the Old School" begins, "Now they have drive-by shootings / while my version is to assassinate the place / by going back and forgiving it for being / so meager." This notion is repeated in "Doubling Up on Privacy at the Canterbury Juvenile Facility."

> What happened to the backyard I once knew,
> the flapping board to the scrap metal heap,
>
> down a street where the flim-flam leanings
> of pre-fabs in wind are whipped nostalgic

And in "The Visit" we see the same theme.

> Whenever I come back, I try not to lead her on.
> I won't take her with me. This is her home:
> this sultry neighborhood, clamped into the
> city . . .
>
> They're floating here until far-away
> children come to rescue them . . .

Is that what the stenographer desires—to be rescued by children? Hardly. But in the sterile world of codes and verbatim transcriptions, the reality of emotions often intrudes, and those intrusions, the rudeness and beauty of images, makes McCue's work both risky and delightful. The stenographer grows from obedient girl, the princess, to prodigal child and, finally, to lover.

> . . . Centered as the news,
> we send out shots like spokes, each alone, each
> beginning here, aiming
> for a far-off place.

That far-off place is reflected in the initial poem, "Astronauts Having Coffee," of Part III, Translation—except now the poet re-visions (looks after) the cliché of the past. Where the joke in "The Stenographer's Breakfast" was no more than "a cup of coffee and a Winston," and "the truth is quick and small / however bright," McCue takes charge in "Astronauts," declaring:

> Give me an astronaut's morning view,
> two cups of coffee upright,
> a plate of fruit, and windows shuttle-wide.

These last poems hold a gathering insistence, a demand for emotions:

> Don't go to sleep
> Stay up with me
> I'll light every lamp
> and throw the chandeliers
> into full swing

In "That Electric Arched Moment," a voice questions authority:

> The romantics had it wrong. Neither the
>   landscape
> nor the sea diagnoses *turbulent* and *calm*
> or mimics what's cheaply psychological.
> What storms we felt were outside ourselves—

McCue's stenographer rails against the structures that confine life, both natural and mechanical, as in "Dead Reckoning" when she argues, "Everyone / I loved who died must have left / the grave like a discarded gift box . . . / This I know / for sure: none of them are in that stinging, / salted earth . . ." And just as she refuses to accept the confines of death, she refuses the confines of roles for the living. She is "the girl who loosened everything," who feared nothing as she "crawled / under sinks, climbed ladders . . ." Her language is, at one and the same time, fluid, ordinary, exalted, spellbinding, grounded, and liberating.

The Stenographer's Breakfast does not offer up a staid world. McCue has not invented the stenographer in order to create poems, rather she has examined those circumstances through which the stenographer, and those like her, can be seen. We have all fallen under the spell of codes: the logos of advertisements, the shorthand of secretaries, the telegrapher's keys, mnemonic devices, computer programs, even 911 are forms of codes designed to make our lives easier, more efficient. With some codes, we have learned to live with chaos. But our accumulation of technological glitter too often reduces our sensitivity to the process of events and our relation to those events. McCue's poems reflect a world in which both order and chaos are revealed as parts of our frantic cavortings. Images scamper across the landscape in poems that are as painterly realistic as a watercolorist's rendition of a landscape, or as surreal as a view in which the landscape is made fluid by a photographer's optical prism. The advantage for the poet is the ability to use language to alter the lens, to change the intensity of details. For McCue, language engages the details and music of the landscape. Her poems are "a yearning for slow motion / or eclipse, one stroke beyond / what's permitted. Casting out toward taboo . . ."

THE
STENOGRAPHER'S
BREAKFAST

I. DICTATION

Secretarial manuals, both aging and current, outline behavior along with the more technical duties of the office. Most guidebooks and Office Mythology presume the stenographer to be a woman with a high school education and a rather rudimentary sense of manners. "It will pay the ambitious stenographer to be consistently cheerful," as "most stenographers are far too sensitive," says Edward Jones Kilduff in *The Stenographer's Manual* (Harper and Brothers, 1921). Taking dictation is her primary role, an essential skill, however difficult the task. Kilduff writes: "If you hold back your dictator, you must practice to develop more speed." By hiring a proficient stenographer, the businessman or politician could assure the memorialization of his words. And since "the good stenographer is loyal to her chief," the secretary must acknowledge the importance of dictation and transcription as her ontology, her source and her starting place. "Whenever you are called by a dictator and do not know if it is for dictation or not, always take your notebook and pencils with you . . . drop all work immediately . . . and go to the dictator's desk."

BORN TO WORK ALONE

The hottest piece of day
and my father's in the den with a rifle
aimed at flies,
shooting up the walls.
But the flies are clever—they move in fronts—
some slow their engines and land behind the couch
where they disguise
themselves as bees. My father thinks they are
retreating, but the flies take off
again, buzzing louder.

As the cowboy takes to corral, trying to think
of the cattle as his
enemy, flanks
tumble off in herds, and for the cowboy,
nixed by nepotism,
how cowardly they are. He swings the chase
through dust and stone;
his cowpoke rope wills
its beholder, surprises collars, stuns

shoulders of cows.
Riveting from his turret, standing on the swivel
chair, my father tries
to match this. What moves,
he shoots: wind, hands of the clock, while lighter
trimmings drop

from shelves: marble,
pen, dried flowers. "Pull," he shouts, and delights
in scaling down the battle,
driving furniture

into air. It hasn't always been like this: Sunday
   morning
paper slapped the floor, diffusing
the smell of coffee through the room,
where scents of pillows still gathered in our hair.
"Get your gun, Annie,"
I think, imagining my father
and me, back to back, taking out every fly
with the windows
open. Centered as the news,
we send out shots like spokes, each alone, each
beginning here, aiming
for a far-off place.

IN SINGLE MOMENTS

Darkness fills the opera as the lead tenor
laments with such resonant formality we are taken
                aback, wishing only
                to articulate mourning
so it would be like this. Remember Buster Keaton running
on the roofs of freight cars, always in the opposite
                direction? The place
                he was pulled from
became another, while the train never knew West, only
the deliberate poles of North and South, passing
                heroines stranded
                in fields or devastated
southern towns—Keaton's china puppet face always cast
without panic. One Easter, three of us
                had to bury
                a cat. In the city,
we had only concrete, construction yards, or the park.
We had children to think of, or the rain
                lifting the cat back
                to us, half-decayed.
This death was a pun or wry little joke: we had particulars
to consider—sweeping the cat from the street
                into a box, finding a patch
                of ground behind a church.
Once the grave was filled, rising before us
like a soft loaf, no one knew what to say.

It was a solemn and funny
occasion, as we were drawn
together over an animal, testing our sympathies, feeling
terrible about it. Tragedy alights in single
moments, containing only
the present, the visible:
a shoe pushed to the back of the closet, a good warm day,
the oxygen tent. Taken away in an ambulance, the woman
who lived on the street
leaves her bag of scraps
behind. The bag remains on the curb, while behind the big top,
the thin man covers the elephant's scars with gray
paint, and the bearded
lady shaves so her whiskers
will grow stronger. Parts of scenes gather
to a bare room. Someone opens a window; you are left alone
with the astonishing breeze filling
the room like cement or dirt.

THE PRINCESS AND THE HIGHWIRE

I. Before She Got to the Circus

What you have is not the greatest
show on earth but misfits howling, a scramble
behind the tents: chicken leg, tassle,
camels loose from cages. The acrobats picnic
before painting their faces.
Animal trainers are fencing, while lions and bears
place bets. Who will tease the elephant today?
But the elephant hazards a guess: "The man with two
noses will win. He rules the ring
whenever he trains, jabbing and poking, and thriving on
pain, again and again and again."

After spearing the thin man, Mr. Two Noses
moves on to bruise the dog, lifting his hoop
higher and higher; the little dog wheedles
through. The dog is brave, following the two-nosed man
to the door of the trailer. Sniffing outside,
he hopes to remind the man of his noses, but the louder
he snorts, the worse it gets: he inhales mud
and glass and paper.

II. How She Got There

His arms as loose as hangers, a man waits at the bottom of the
    stairs,
tiptoeing back and forth.

"I may never come down. I won't," she says. (They'd sold her
to the circus.)

The man circles the house. He drops the corsage. He doesn't
remember her name.

The cast calls, longs for a princess. Without her, the show
cannot go on.

III. She Arrives at the Circus

Enter the princess with fire
extinguisher. After putting out
the smoking frog, she turns
into a wavering child,
a leather cloud, symphony.

The princess skirts
center stage
sings like rain
notes boomerang
from bleachers sopped
in sawdust

IV. What Happened Then

The princess gave up her status, married into
the loose limbs of the thin man,
flew the trapeze, courted
the net which tangled her
heart. Folded in rain tents

behind the big top, the net stood her up
on Sunday matinees. Relentlessly, the princess
flirted—below her, only ground
and a loitering elephant
gazing up—a little
saddle on his back.

                    a board breaks
                                in the bleachers
                    rasping sounds
                                filling out the blues
                    falsetto
                                she drops from the bar
                    curved body like moon

                                        The princess had me
                                        I am her son and
                                        you need to know
                                        the trapeze leads
                                        my mother
                                        not anchored by
                                        tent or stands
                                        tough eye swinging
                                        I call to her
                                        must you must you must
                                        Mother
                                        She swoops gently
                                        as a waiter's hand
                                        encore met
                                        piles of costumes
                                        I was born here

V. Each Nook of the Circus

tells a different part: the princess
came from the suburbs.
No, she came from the ghetto.
My father is the thin man who plays
the wires—No, he is the man with two noses.
"When did the princess have me?"
echoes this place where dreaming children

are banished, where all is only possible:
boy with one leg, hacksawed
self, or young man with three eyes,
gift of a tent stake, or littlest Houdini
who never got out,
embalmed, propped up, and kept in a case.
What can I be without talent, unscarred and here?
This is no dress rehearsal. I feed
the animals ice cream, and bucket the trimmings.
My job is to look after things.

AUNT LILLIAN, THE CHEMIST AND
THE MAGICIAN

Simple twists of dustrag and broom,
Aunt Lillian swept her rooms clean
as adjoining tombs. In the pharmacy
below, the chemist eyedropped cures
or addictions, she couldn't be sure.

Each conjured order but never
enough: the downstairs druggist wavered
over paper where litmus molecules
danced in rings. He topped the bottles
with cotton—enough so a genie

could breathe. Upstairs, resourceful Aunt Lil
found the magician in the yellow pages
when she looked under *maids,*
How tidy a magician would be—
He'd whisk the steaming pans to cupboards,

juggle mothballs from cedar chests
as her clothes folded seam to seam, midair.
Wind flushes hall and stair—and there—
the magician guides a wheelbarrow packed
with props. He tips hats, rabbits

and scarves to the floor, as the wheelbarrow
collapses to the size of a keyboard,
a tiny tabletop. A boy really, he clicks

his hightops under the garlic braids;
twine starts to unwind; the cloves fly

unskinned to the skillet.
Aunt Lil's rooster teapot steams from the beak.
Surprised by such urbanity, Aunt Lil
watches the boy turn and pepper her rooms:
a brass bed appears, palm trees block

the coal-smudged windows, a cat struts
from rug to rug. Astonished,
she can only wait, but what the magician
has in mind is dictating fate, and furnishing
what Aunt Lillian strains to keep bare.

Finally, after he sprinkles the walls
with paintings and mirrors, she orders
him to make these distractions vanish.
Just an apprentice, he hasn't learned
the spell to undo his genesis,

and dismayed, the boy removes his hat,
trolleys his things away.
Without him, the room deflates.
Lamps shrivel to pivots like stars
or peepholes. In the dark, she calls him back,

and checks the stair, as if glaring
down a microscope long unfocused. There
the chemist pours his last solution
for the night. A somber iodine escapes,
defies his walls, spirals up to Aunt Lil's room

where a spot appears, blemish-tinged, too late
for the boy magician. Seizing bolts of cloth
still waiting for her gown, the stain
is her placebo tested here—in the long struggle
for the ordinary to promptly disappear.

IN A TOWN NOT FAR FROM HERE:
SPEECHES FROM THE MAYOR'S OFFICE

I. Photo Opportunity

As the mayor, I am for tourists, but no brochure would
bring them here. There's the charm! No RV parks or
campsites. We believe in rain. We like to stay
indoors. There are few expenses. City employees are
paid to maintain atmosphere. Mostly, they whittle.
I play the banjo on the porch and wait
for my reelection. Industry? We have a golfball
factory. Machine-wrapped string cores, and the tiny
pores are all discharged in the river. Hardest thing
about this town: the compost problem. Some folks don't
know the difference between fertilizer and trash. One
rots, one consoles—same as people or memories.

II. Motion and Necessity

Newspaper lines the desert, flagstones to our glass
mosaic of city streets where a man tightens his
hands behind his back, hiding handcuffs from his son.
The father moves backward against traffic, which
constantly passes away. (There is not a toll over
the bridge leaving town, since this bald-faced mayor
encourages departure.) No role model for his boy,
we asked the father to go, but like all those who see

life as closure's prophecy, the father loves the bridge, dreams it, but can never cross it: his cell inherits the spires of its suspension. Fascinated, his son watches planes take off at the airport. The son adores all manners of moving things. Both back up against stasis, locked into its vortex, pushed outward.

III. When the Old Mayor Returned to the
Private Sector

(1) *Which is easier, planting tulips or waiting for daffodils!* (2) *When is respect more justified—for the policeman drunk at the annual ball or for the dog catcher's record-setting day!* (3) *Who is older, someone dead for years or Mr. Snowly—just turned 94!* When I came into office, the citizens were speechless, flailing through days as they had the mayorless cluster before: lonely in humility, unwavering in their strife. The process speaks. I am here to save them.

When the old mayor retired, the townspeople lifted their clocks overhead and went to church. Thistle clean, that mayor was ascetic and trustworthy as a short-sleeved magician. No one could replace him. The citizens waited and waited for decisions to be rendered, but without the mayor, they stacked up fast. His stenographer, forced to write each dilemma on a separate slip, pierced requests through some old receipt spindles, and lined them on the village green. Weeks passed. Townsfolk got tired of going to church, tired of watching the papers pinch into blooms, growing like sunflowers. One by one, they knelt before the spindles. Each citizen tore off a dilemma:

Jailed tailors design styles both vogue
and functional: take your work to them.

Do not fall in love with your own stitches
or your drawers will fill

with string and cotton.
Should you use the word "monogamy," *home*

will become an ark of singulars: one lamp,
one fork, one chair, an unlit

candlestick. Before removing them,
assure the banished

a comfortable waiting room. If you
bring *earth* and *sky* together

beware of dust storms. Fear
loosens holy stones and erodes

seraphim. Turn toward it,
welcoming yourself back

into a world both large and dim,
where nothing glimmers in excess.

TRAVELING NORTH BY CAR
PAST THE SPOON FACTORY

Crossing the lake, it rained until
air swelled into damp cotton
stuffing the car like our closet
where clothes mingled
scents for months. By the time the two of us
reached country beyond
swamp, the air was of sheep
and lambs lingered

like dandelions.
Outside town, a man
shirtless in his hoe-down overalls,
shoulders his boots
home. Trailing behind, a woman lifts
the rods and fish. Somehow, she keeps
them from crossing in her arms
the way poles do
once out of water: rods divined
to tangle, to point out the landscape's
errant poles. This faulty compass
detects a magnet there:
the old spoon factory. As a girl,
the woman recalls, piles of dust
whistled behind the place.
The river glistened by, catching shards

like flies or leaves. Now the rapids tuck
themselves farther back, folding into the crux
of mountains, solid as spoons.

The city's foundation comes down
to this: body-bag plastics,
leftover wrap-ups, jumps
from kitchens to curbs,
transitions escaping us.
We try and leave gracefully.

I imagine statues, hunkering down—
atavistic and sincere,
as if folks lived below
the chiselings of their clothes.
Your hands trail curves, jump stations in the air,
imitating scenery, and other inaccuracies.
Somewhere behind this backdrop
birdcatchers flock to nets, and hermits
tend their garden greens. Meanwhile,
in a land no longer there, this is the hour
when the phone rings, the hour water boils.

INTERVIEW WITH THE HANGMAN

What are your qualifications? Describe your job history.

I apprenticed with the best.
Back alley shootings, the junkie's last fix—
always there to tie somebody off. The end
to death's delays, I worked behind paramedic

and strangler, next to the embalmer
(too often honored as the immaculate, tidy one).
Got my start on rats, moved on to dogs, wired up
those cars my mother's jealous lovers had. I've been at it

without the black hood's awning, just a plain face
ready to poison what needed it.
Not just a skill, being the killer of killers,
it's a matter of integrity. Such a sweet meadow,

the calm after twitches and gags.
Relief, that is my history.

What are your long term goals?

If the past is a sweep, the future's a slow
lease on an empty back forty.
The long-term goal is some hussock
where grasses tip the field. From here, I can see
my contribution—little sweat, tirade without

expression. To execute with the cool hand
of a programmer, I aim, then feel
the world as a series of knobs
or switches waiting for the flip by one
who knows no in-between, doesn't believe
the limp hair or wretching ribs
are human. I'll be just another
instrument to penetrate a system,
graveside. Ending life to tell life
how it will be.
You need to sneak up
and not predict.
Anything worthwhile is secret.

How devoted are you?

Reliable as the rope, the needle, and the chair.
I'll stand as a runner at the gate,

the prince before coronation.
As ready to accept

punishment as to dole it out. The anxious part
is building up: last words, last meal,

end to endings. I fear jumping
the gun. Or the hesitation the whole world

prays for: the understudy running on
too soon, too delighted—the old actor still on stage.

I'll wait, no need to overpower anyone.
Death row's a lemonade stand.

Lines lengthen and the painful part, the wait.
Relax. I am the end itself.

The line.

THE SINKING, THE IRRETRIEVABLE

We'd rather have the iceberg than the ship.
   —*Elizabeth Bishop*, "The Imaginary Iceberg"

Photographs hold it—the ship turning
from frigate to iceberg, then
only the open aperture of iceberg.

For years, attention swells
from sinking to survivors
until news of a discovery washes ashore.

Like the fuss before a hurricane,
instruments collect, and archeologists
hooded in slickers gather

around old fishing boats. Here,
the landlocked consider the lost
as simply the uncharted:

Jetties line the sturdy harbor.
Lamps are left on.
The voyage begins a replication.

Bows tipped, the fleet points
to the marked desert of water,
gesturing ahead, anxious for artifacts.

Underneath, jilting beams poke through
portholes, spotting glasses never
quite tipped, filled and floating

while the thin sound of depth
accompanies this descent into the past,
and the air of the living

rises. No wreck here, no museum
of human remains or any other.
This chandeliered grave of coral

settles as the sea
is her moat, a castle irretrievable
where softly, geology begins.

SOUNDMAKER:
THE DICTATOR'S SCENARIO

Under a hanging microphone,
a man rumbles sheet-metal
into wind, crushes a cellophane
downpour, and tips a pair of heels
across the tabletop in his fists:
he orders a woman home in the rain.

Behind shades of the radio's
netting and wood, the dissonance-maker
leads the woman, mounted on her horse,
through the dining room—
knocking walnuts to wood.
Outside, he tunes to wind and haymowers:
The woman stands in an open field.

Dreaming, the soundman hears a car start
and roll away, but it is only the settling
hum of the refrigerator. An obese king
in vestments like bedsheets
whistles as he trots his little dog—mitten
on a string. In this kingdom, sirens whine
as the sheriff steps from his car,
his dusty star hidden
in the folds of his outback

jacket. *Where is the woman?* He listens
for her, but hears only the rustling of waking

dying soundmakers. Lining the man's closets
with patch-puffs of quilts soaked
in the rain, small fields swell
to the till. Train whistles, foghorns,
and the woman's tipsy laugh
move through his shutters, funneling
into the china doorknob of a closet where
a tiny orchestra plays on the shelves,
beckoning: *You can come in,*
You can make this music.

II. TRANSCRIPTION

Having a method to transcribe the Important Words in politics or business implied that order could be maintained, that records could be kept, and that words had a literal effect upon the culture. *Stenography* is now an archaic term for mechanized phonetic shorthand; today you will meet only court reporters, not stenographers. The machines, however, have not changed much since they were patented in 1910: twenty-three faceless black keys in the shape of fingers are mounted on a tripod stand. Like shorthand, *steno* is a reductionist language of symbols encoding vowel and consonant sounds. When played in combination, the keys designate particular sounds, depending on the phoneme's location within a word. The stenotypist, or court reporter, keys the phonemes while the machine generates a tape of symbols. Because the machine works with *sounds*, and not the intellectual process of coding by *meaning*, the procedure is as fast as it is accurate. Like playing the piano, transcription flows from the ear, through the hands, into chords, and the art grows quickly intuitive.

THE STENOGRAPHER'S BREAKFAST

I.

Legs pinched together, I play the machine
sidesaddle, fingers bobbing from the keys like I'm pulling
laundry from a trough. History dictates
such wrong-headed order which I *digest*,
resuscitate as *skill, employ*—a wry design
to sit off-center and transcribe
roomfuls of men, their ties loosened,
interrogating the next of kin.

Aside: *To take dictation* means I watch each speak,
turn my face, read lips and leap—*space*—

from one to the other.
Today there are three of them.
Across the table, a widow props her body up,
answering as she can.
When they called me here
to conference table, stiff-backed chair,
I dedicated my serving them as a prayer
for this woman. I prepared

to be the voyeur, the silent ear,
the widow's distillery of truth and relay.
The government of such a room—

Never stop the proceedings. Speak when spoken to.—
prevents an active defense. What this group of men
delivers is some quest for accuracy,
but I know this technique
depends on the distance between man and paper,

chair and door, woman and her role.
All this talk might well have been
over a telegraph, the way the tap-tap clicks
and bounces back. The lawyers only call the widow in
so they may watch her eyes and face
to find, by chance, if she wished her husband dead.
In a skirt, ascot-necked and jacket
tight, I blend right into them, take my place and offer

Shorthand: a lack, understaffed, decoding and
recoding, carrying language to its core.

And more—the world of facts brought to bear
on whatever questions they ask of her.
Your husband, did he provide for you?
The day he died, what was it that he wore?
I'll revive it later, fill the gaps.
Umm hmm. Cough. Cough. included as the manual says.
Such faith I have in sounds not yet
formed as words, shy riddles and intrusions

into code. *Interruptions are difficult*
but essential to include in any transcript.

II.

Clerk smart, each step parts my raincoat
as if I'm crossing through brambles
or over tracks. This is the walk from the office
when the keypunch and earphones

shinny down my bones, and patter skin.
Not long, and I can't distinguish between my own
footfall and the street, my eye from market
or kiosk—I can't help transcribing

everything. *The curb stiffens like a brow.*
Cars unscrew the pavement. Time releases
the tower's clock from its confines.
A back alley considers revealing some trauma,
my reason for clipping forward. And the walls,
what do they reflect, as wainscot and gargoyle
lift to frame my stroll?
Even these coordinates weaken to arcs,

tease my decoding mind—
flit of paper, twirl of can.
Today, taking dictation from the men,
word by word, I took the widow's life,
pushed its tiny pulse through the chords.
After the flush of pity, I could only be
stoic. And tomorrow, as I translate
those symbols, the marks like stray hairs

on the tickertape—they will spell out phrases:
I don't know. He just stopped breathing.
There's nothing else to say.
He turned blue.
And the pinched sobs, to chart as stage directions,
what the manual dictates as *the witness cries,*
or in some other case, *the witness gestures,*
the witness faints.

You know the joke: The Stenographer's Breakfast
is a cup of coffee and a Winston. On the bare stage

with table and placemat, the secretary
empties her life before she goes into work.

When I reach the stairs
and my rooms, even the absent-minded move,
a nod to the dog, flip of the light switch
is some calculated truth. I document the area,
and think how heaven must be some version
of a waiting room—the widow's husband

lingering on a cloud-swollen couch.
Here in my walk-up,
I can look out to a sky
blown into dome by breath
while somewhere overhead
Galileo milks the stars
one at a time.
Like my keys, his notes

test the pure relay of truth,
but the truth is quick and small
however bright. And in this time
when each place is earmarked
by hordes, purity frustrates me
as heaven does. How can I help
loving the chronological
seductions of file and box?
Imagine the alternative chaos.

DOCTOR DOCTOR

When sleep is sultry, ham-hock sweat
to nose and mouth, the surgeon of insomnia sets
the bones—work endowed by human rumblings,
folding in armless and enormous. He's never lost
a patient, even with pills. Without
a white coat, but sporting wing tips
dusty as cats, the surgeon jolts

ahead, keeping the patient wide-eyed.
Raid on bedclothes, he stirs this woman
awake: Turn up the heat. Chug the wind.
But who keeps the surgeon up, alert and sinewy?
Untimely precision—a graveyard shift dismantling
sleep with such clear slices: wake wake wake-up
This is a house call. We're losing time.

Now they have drive-by shootings
while my version is to assassinate the place
by going back and forgiving it for being
so meager. How we walked these little worlds
like flea markets, our dimes palmed,
assembling relief beneath tree-slapped eaves.
There once, we touched each other's chests
to see if leftover smoke rattled within us.

I came back to get what I had of you.
But any trip here would shoot us both
closer to myth, like some old Bendix
rusting to poppies. Sure enough, on the way
I passed a yard—tomato plants blooming from
    the washer,
bleached-out sneakers hung from the line.

For Mark Webster

DOUBLING UP ON PRIVACY AT THE CANTERBURY JUVENILE FACILITY

What happened to the backyard I once knew,
the flapping board to the scrap metal heap,

down a street where the flim-flam leanings
of pre-fabs in wind are whipped nostalgic

as a Walt Disney movie? And the cinderblock
discount outlets, where *faith upheld* is a delivery

halfway here? Escaping the bolted trailers
and free-throw lots wasn't enough:

a neighborhood in this place contains five kids
huddled over a cigarette near a mess hall dumpster.

Most of us are sixteen. The faculty is Catholic
but *Salvation*'s leaving

on the next Peter Pan bus to Hartford.
We might be a million miles off—

or here, cramped in some school without recess,
in dormitories with cots and cardboard bureaus.

You can only read and write between seven and nine.
No more than five can gather at a time. No two alone.

That's why we're digging this hole with a smuggled,
folding shovel. In a thick flock of trees it's growing

big as a grounded spaceship. Dirt on the edges patted
flat as a dollar, we climb in,

pull the branches overhead, pair off slowly
hand to thigh, and think how

when we leave this place for good
we'll pile into some car like we do

this hole. Across the beer-smudged dark,
my friend Peter says, "It's good enough to die in."

Then: the flashlight through the woods, tearing through,
ripping like a freeway—my life, a stint between flashes—

From there on: any light head-on is blinding.
I can't hold it clear—but together, doubled up

here, when we all go, we'll know—
We drank. We drove.

LANDMARKS AS RANDOMLY
FIXED POINTS

No yearbook could ever get it right:
my father faded into 1960
swollen-lipped and smug,
one boy like the rest, warmed by
the page's fold. I marked his place
with yarn—a tiny morgue with sheets
thrown back, drawers pulled open.

Through a hinge or doorjamb
I'd catch some shift in air,
and think of him unclaimed
somewhere—on a train platform
his newspaper bridled, ornery in his fists,
tie askew, clamped in the wrong shoes.

He was a whole town misplaced,
too far to reach. What memories could I
have of absence? No maps existed,
and the villages grew
burdened with stoplights and storefronts
I wasn't there to see. Or I confused
him with the town crier, cocksure and smart,

the one who patrolled the maze
his joints crunching through streets
aging so fast, I couldn't keep up,
couldn't be sure I recognized them.

Maybe my father did stand
city-locked upon platforms

dizzy with the erotic steer
of trains pulling in, or easy
in the eye's hot rustle of cowboy rope,
secured in some mangy corral.
Since loss is not an error in navigation,
but the random earmark, the turned page,

if we met deep in the world, or now,
I'd turn him back, then step away—
our boots tipping off
in the pure shudder of a windless day.

LIVING WITH TRANSCRIPTION

Humidity gathers to the screens.
Slow sidewalks reel me in,
and whisked into life behind
the retina, several times removed,
I watch my grandmother—
a girl of sixteen—leaving New Orleans.
   Or leaning into this candid of her
   in 1920, swept through boundaries
   so trim, I am her child's child
   elbowing in. Amidst the station's pace,
   I'm platform-steady, half-hidden in her coat.
   Borders of the photograph collapse,
lapsing to my grandmother's station
in days when geography
was synonomous with kin,
and ladies never left
their heritage. How great and near
those gaps in lineage are!
   Our lives sway from metacenters,
   once buoyant, as the railway steams.
   Forgive me here while I hanker up
   an accent, reproduce it further
   into a parabiotic world.
   Transcription so dear a passage
passes to adopted ones. So spin
the helix, join the romp in code!

Landscapes center us, we think,
but we are stand-ins of ourselves.
Around each of us, like clothing
on the floor, discarded—
                cards thrown down the night before—
                other lives we know so well
                but never touch, they hide in impulse,
                in gestures left. And when the swift night
                burns over you, the dog howls,
                and someone's at the door, you'll dress
to address a world unknown to you
before: trains, timetables,
her pointed shoes and hat,
a hapless blend of what's recorded.
The real story's caught one slant back:
that wink forever caught behind the eye.

THE TEXT BURIED IN THE WRECK

*Most unfortunate of all conquistadors, Pánfilo de
Narvaez lost two ships in a hurricane, and landed
somewhere on the Gulf coast of Florida. . . . There he
built a fleet of boats with spikes fashioned from spurs
and stirrups, rigged with cordage and sails made from
the hull and hides of horses eaten by his men. In those
crazy craft he sailed past the mouth of the Mississippi,
only to be wrecked on the coast of Texas.*
　　　—*Samuel Eliot Morison,* Oxford History of the
　　　American People

After the Vikings' hi-jinx, these boats
were flank-steady as they spurred and startled
the gullet of the gulf, but it was history
whose hurried sheets buried you, Pánfilo,

not cordage and spleen rocked into the coast.
"Believe, believe," you tried to say,
"Filet those horses, twine the tendrils
then pull the bones and lock with pegs."

Delicate work, raising clods to buoyancy;
no more throttle in those hooves. Hide-wrapped
hulls were bellies alive again.
Imagine the fate unread: racked ribs

and split hides whistled into brittle carriages
on willow wheels—the lovely clacking of skulls
and timber across a tinderbox desert.
In search of spices once again, your crew

labored on. So much energy in such desperation!
Your last fling was carefully planned.
How were you to know the landscape
would sweep from poisoned tropics

to barren hinterland? Consider where I am:
rounded bandits linger behind
dogfood factories, and truth is a ballad
of shards rewound from a jukebox.

Take heart, Pánfilo, decorum is as vital
to the passage as the mechanisms are.
Your horses were nautical, and you the admiral
corralled in whim. Since history will never lie

enough to get it right, spend your time in legend
thinking of those horses—how you set sail
by the twine of corded innards and the spikes—
spurs urging, kicking the wind along.

There's no room for you here—they're crossing
the Atlantic in dinghies and balloons.
Crawl back inside those generous lives—
Those hides, they saved you once.

THE VISIT

Whenever I come back, I try not to lead her on.
I won't take her with me. This is her home:
this sultry neighborhood, clamped into the city

like a gym locker. Doorjamb geraniums
leak to the cobblestones;
oregano burns on the sill. Traffic slows

to the steadiness of flies. Out back,
my mother sighs to the neighbors
from her lawn chair. Print dresses

rolling like shower curtains, the other ladies swing
around her in the street, settling in.
From the window, I can't help watching

this little pram of survivors,
these widows strung along the sidewalk,
tacked to their chairs: bobbing and waiting.

They're floating here until far-away
children come to rescue them, and their tiny
apartments. How they each would gloat,

carried off alone by a son or daughter—
the other women no more filler
than a lamp, a radio, an old book.

As for my mother, well, she would miss
the summer in Little Italy, a parade
every weekday, and evenings, the Holy Roller

ice cream truck: rocket popsicles
and a lesson in Jesus. Folding shirts
into a suitcase, I'm ready to leave

on one train too many, while her anger
strains behind me, sure as a dozen eggs—
plainly stored, secure.

ETIQUETTE

Dunoon, Scotland

Thin as an umbrella rib, my grandmother
clacked into the bakery. Even the untidy
flour seemed miserable, dishonest to her sniff—
fleeing to corners. Her eye snared each
pastry hoarding some puffy secret: icing tarred
the cakes; little knives slunk in the popovers.
This bread is like furniture. And she took
my hand, pulling me from the shimmering
bakery cases, loaves strangled from meathooks,
and the painful pies, bleeding to their pans.

The day they carried her out, I was bending
over her garden. Released, the winded flowers
marched to their borders: little heads of steer,
stubborn and slow. Wrapped in her dinner linens,
she was still angled, seated as she was
by the phone, borne across the lawn. How happy
I was seeing her twirled up in her own
etiquette, in *those cloths we save for company.*

Room to room, house to yard, they shouldered
the debris: hat boxes, crystal vases, needlepoint
stools. Could I forget the sour peach
rooms, the outlets spidered up like scrambling
hesitations, last minute hurls to the wall?
The spoiled rugs, glass cabinets, unused chairs?
These things are worth something.

But what she preserved had already gone by:
exhausted lamps, her own wrung-out life—
all as obsolete as wedding china.

I'll be honest. I don't have any
respect for the dead; I'll whisper after them
and feel daring. Memory, really, is no
more aperture-powered than the oven door:
Open it and the cake will fall.
Photographs will never make her any lighter,
so how happy I am she'll finish out the rot
below ground—how happy I am that soon,
there will be nothing of her at all. Just some
tingle or maxim rising suddenly, and I can't wait
for the years to wash it by, little by little:
the slow yawns of the restless yonder.

BARN RAISING

The clouds stand
like dark stones
over the frame of our
new barn, anchored
to the hill
holding the bay.
We are still
new together, lifted
here by whim
to each
hollow and wisp
of hay, driving
nails faster, watching
them disappear into wood
like lost intentions.
The neighbors have gone,
leaving only scraps
for roofbeams;
you hammer block chips
filling gaps, looking
as strong as when
we started. Your paint-
smeared cap brings
only its immediate
brim while

on the other ladder
I pause as wind
kicks in and dinghies
gather
wooden and solemn
to a far-off pier.

WHAT CAN BE RETAINED

In the harbor, late
the cable stays of sailboats
ring against metal masts,
a song arranged
by wind. This same

breeze rushes through
you, leaves without one
measured bar, or the memory
of one thick note to hum.

And when the gale turns
sharply to sea, seducing
waves into whitecaps
you think: white-on-blue,
white-on-blue, dipping
your crude brush

into a wash murky as the rise
and fall of blues
blending to gray. Melody
of the harbor breaks
into gentle clatter.
As you imitate, you recall

an old myth: every time you
draw breath too deeply
your heart stops.

III. TRANSLATION

I soon forgot storm in music.
—*Charlotte Brontë*, Jane Eyre

The desire to record speech may evolve from the human yearning to hold memory in place, to replay events, and to document wisdom and confession without distortion. Translating a dialogue or dictator's monologue from tape to script locks the interaction into the present, giving it the illusion of accuracy. The process, however, is full of loopholes where truth can wriggle free. At its best, translation becomes a precise *attempt* to reproduce the language spoken. According to Kilduff, "Good transcribing means much more than the accurate typing of stenographic notes," as if innuendo, inflection, and initiative finally might have a place in the rigorous system of good translation. The gap between obeying instructions (taking dictation) and living resourcefully (translating to text) is the stenographer's source of creation, and even survival. While she constructs antidotes to the chaos of language loose in the air, our chipper Della Street-turned-Girl Friday secretly thrives on the distortions therein.

ASTRONAUTS HAVING COFFEE

The orbs, the trifles, Galileo's ruffled brow—
whatever spins this world along so
trembling in her sky, I'd love the glimpse,
some proof our world's askew,
moving us through this corridor of dust and space.
Give me an astronaut's morning view,
two cups of coffee upright,
a plate of fruit, and windows shuttle-wide.

Say there are two
of us, anchored in atomic suits,
gloves outstretched, big as nets.
We can't decide what is ripe.
Does the fruit here hold a different hue?
Does a peach remain a peach in space?
There is no right side up, and even
time's aligned without progression.
Fruit here, will never be suitable to eat.

Mid-swoop, gravity is a cage flung wide.
Floating feels disorganized.
The coffee's not so good, and
as an astronaut, I feel misled by chaos,
but have a sense there's ghostly more:
Could space be space
without the earth below?

Does the planet take someone watching
just to make it go?

Room for two, we hardly make a dent
and I wonder if space has a patron saint—
some astronaut who needed proof,
but came upon the unlikely truth
that coffee leaves you tense
and expanse too broad is not a view.
What I tell my partner through
our wired-up suits
is that we are someone else's

view: a lonely, weightless nick against the dark,
like a boy I once loved on a theater rooftop.
When we kissed, a cigarette toppled
from his grip, and we flicked
our eyes to the small untended star
sparkling down, flipping for the crowd.

WHAT'S DANGEROUS ABOUT PLUMBING

For weeks, that waterline
held gravity's wings
and refused to leave
the ceiling for the floor.
Above, I walked the edges of my rooms.
What would it take to torque
the thing? One loose doorbell,
some plant's twitch? All dangers
smooth as pins—imagine the silt
once the flood soaked in!
The wires, hanging ready,
urge the pipe to drop;
they'll need only one
wet spark. I could have fixed it then:
the girl who loosened everything,
saw pipes and fiddled
with the bolts. Nothing
scared me when I crawled
under sinks, climbed ladders;
I'd hitch the pipe up and go
heavy through the house.
The problem here I think
is knowing how the pipe will blow
ahead of time. Any minute now
I'm sure—there's no time
to get the tools. Uneven currents

crackle through the walls
as the pipe meanders
under floorboards, drips.
Comes the moment when
I wish it would flip
its shackles, give the house
a shudder, let me fire up
the pumps, and splash by splash,
go headlong, then recover.

ACCORDING TO NEO-PHYSICS

the Noosphere is *thought*'s outer
layer, sealed around the globe,
way out beyond the ozone.
Each fantasy and algebraic
function rises up
and gathers there. All joined
in a pact to think
nothing, could we exacto-slice
windows through the density,
just to have a peek?

Success! Stars pull near.
It lasts until some philosopher
takes charge. His diagrams,
thick with thoughts, cover the glimpses
we designed, and stretch into a cone
far overhead. The great greenhouse
grows a dunce cap. Telescopes realigned,
the dilemma is to focus
narrowly, jotting imitations,
or to imagine what's out there:

ideas gathering around us
like mortar or cotton, with spikes
scattered, aloof and stubborn—
jutting through
the over-worked air.

Cowls of stone, floor and stair
folded to the door, the tower leans away
from the peasant house; another day,
and it shades thatch. Beneath

the tower—trim sieve above water—
the river slows. He waits
for staples: the delivery wagon-loaded down
a one-wagon-road. Inside, sword and shoelace

prepare the miniature hanging: two hairs line
a spectator's guardrail, and the Rosicrucian wake:
dead mouse by the fireplace. So close
to where he sleeps and writes, elders waver

red-eyed above his head. Preparing his event,
he scrubs the kitchen, stocky and hot, cuts
the flowers, props the mouse. The elder
    communicators
do approve of how this guest can manage solitude:
sacraments in the castle's tower, clutching peasant
    house.

LULLABY

Don't go to sleep
Stay up with me
I'll light every lamp
and throw the chandeliers
into full swing
Let's pop some fuses
Up up up   your mouth's gone
slack   agape
Go akimbo like I am
The foot of the bed
unhappy bench
here's the newspaper
fallen from your hand
Come on read me the headlines
But the bearings of your eyes
they roll   You're warm
and slow   Wake up   It's cold
we're playing hearts
your deal
An all night diner?
I'll start the car
You're missing this
storing yourself up
Quit dreaming
There's a place
inside you I can't go

Get up
I'll pinch your toes
Now you'll twitch
but try the sprawl
standing up
The radio   I'll turn it on
There
Don't you admire this song?
Near water or night
the far-off is near
Roll over
No stop there
Being tired
a snare and all this sleep
intrudes   it gets used
to you and warms your feet
seals the sheets
Love is ever so lonesome
I'll retreat

SIMPLE DISTORTIONS

Plants tip
in half-light, dull the kitchen's
still-life: egg-sized grapes
sink into a china plate.

Stale mezzanine
of *home*, this man's white hand goes
cold in his breast
pocket. Mouth wide, he oversees

bugs in rice. Were he alive,
this inversion might remind him of
"WORLD'S LARGEST CANTALOUPE AND TOMATO"
tough as towels

or songs. In his kitchen, a calendar—
distorted by its rules:
nothing inhabited, nothing gained.
Everything grows beyond its means.

DEAD RECKONING

Frigates crawl near, thunder cursed, kneeling
through the over-charted water.
Each trawler takes on rust, rejects paint,
whines under her own syrup-slow
foghorn. I come to the docks to watch passages
more predictable than my own:
the scheduled apogees of a port-to-port life,
freight hauled and weighed
under skies dank as crematoriums, humid too.
What kicks around after
every move: root, pear, brown-buckle boots,
the sandpaper innards of bottomfish.
Such below-decks wreckage turns arctic in the mind.
Cranes whir and rise,
trolley up the winter's fish in frozen lockers.
When I squint, follow the hoists,
there's the swell of a hundred dream-locked breaths
from rattled bunks—
the sweet riffs of wheezing cows, healing in snowbound fields,
forgiving the drought.
Tunnel-still, the ships echo after each unloading,
as if they were lifting out
each body I once knew in those frozen lockers. Everyone
I loved who died must have left
the grave like a discarded gift box, and secretly slipped
back into the world. This I know

for sure: none of them are in that stinging,
salted earth, tucked
in some fleece-lined cemetery. Grandmother, Dad, lover,
   friend—
they are all out there,
taking on other itineraries, and I'm just missing
their ports of call.
Thousands of alibis mingle on the docks, and here I am
wasting another day, parking
under the causeway, trying to decide where to jump in,
when to join them.

"THAT ELECTRIC ARCHED MOMENT"

After a line by Mark Webster

The romantics had it wrong. Neither the landscape
nor the sea diagnoses *turbulent* and *calm*
or mimics what's cheaply psychological.
What storms we felt were outside ourselves—
somewhere else. Our boots beat down the grasses,
mud-first slides into the bog,
your hunt and then the ducks—I was gun shy—
and the dog—he pulled us safely home.

And later: a boy and girl out in the reeds,
our voices muted in the rain, the clench
of thighs and bowels to lead us someplace warm.
But the weather's hidden patterns
were not enough to rule our hearts.
Four hands against the wind, we pinned map to tree,
but the map still rolled and creased.
We trudged into its folds, and found a trail.

Somewhere in a hidden pleat is where you must be now.
Truth be told, I just can't muster up
how I get to you, so I reach around corners and become
    inclined
to love what's inorganic. Your clothes fill
old trunks once bound for college, but the geography of you
goes placeless in my mind. Evenings drop
so heavy, even my sleepless dreams turn colorblind.
I keep track of letters and your laugh,

cynical and warm. You are every object's dormancy,
every action's gesture
possibly implied. I feel your death hands on.

This is not an elegy but an acappella in-between,
a limbo rag where the music improvises
each crescendo leap like your heart
the day it gave its final heave.
Any repertoire that has enough repeats—
one might call a *crash* a *beat*
like the springless synapse
when the vein constricts
and your heart stopped flow.
But where is all that music supposed to go?

I promise to prune the tree that blocks the barn
and keep the lofts and stalls from taking over the farm
by lightning splinter and collapse.
A cracked sky already fluctuates rain
and I imagine our unrestored ceiling as your rickety floor—
you and the other dead clustered there.
This lurch, this linchpin lands me in that morning
when convulsions sent you blue, then gray.
I have a million *why, why not* visions of this climb
to find you. A relief map moors
our world, fixes points of detail—What's bearable.
I deprive myself of sense to find the route.

BY TWO

HE: Light settles sheets to limbs. I awake first
to her skin, afraid my rougher touch may
bruise her soft linen of sleep, a white land
she circles with shaded eyes—tenement
roofs where Billie Holiday is humming
so loudly no one hears the traffic.

SHE: Where I am, shots topple brick. A train roars
from the closet through this crumpled map—
limbo. Stretched, picked clean, and laid in a long
white box, my arms dangle like flaccid ropes,
awaiting the magician who will part
my body, draw it aside and pass through.

Something washes ashore. Minister and midwife
lift their cloaks, trembling toward the wake.

DILEMMA

My towel draping the basin, and naked,
I'm thinking of past lovers,
old books, and the rhythm of my work:
loose whispers through breast and toe.
Cotton strokes the window sill
and scents the steam.
I wait for water to hold
its wake and drop degrees.

Am I but a system of canals, inveterate
and stale? Pressed to desk and phone,
or taking steno, am I dictation's instrument
fostered at the CAREER GIRL's store?

What's erotic to men may not be
a woman's provocation.
Afternoon's dim nostalgia, the tacit invitation:
my body wavering between this hot day
filling the tub, and a yearning for slow motion
or eclipse, one stroke beyond
what's permitted. Casting out toward taboo,
words that won't quite translate,
I crave such lapses—

the drain sucking, and my arms
like serifs curling, sweeping,
while water licks the edges.

THE WAY YOU DESCRIBE IT

Who wouldn't love a washed frame warehouse
where seventy panes of glass align the view
of a molten freeway, headed south?

And the woman you found there—
her ears so slight and sharp, the sun
spears red through them—who wouldn't be

her lover? Of course you move in, and listen
to the seamstresses one floor up,
pedal the clickity up-downs of bobbins

whirring themselves blind.
Any letter is an account gone slant,
Say whatever you like. She is purity, this woman

who livens up your rooms. No man lingers
inside her. She'll bring you that disappearance
lovers feel, when the body leaves the skin

and travels in. Try this: two by two the world awakes,
millimeters from each other's faces, so big, so wide
one isn't sure what lingers there, inside

the other. But the two of you—her womb, like yours,
a tiny bulge concealed, a blessed hoard
less like the warehouse than what it stores.

Printed in the United States
by Baker & Taylor Publisher Services